T0208428

LOVING
People
WELL

Linda Rykowski, M.S., L.C.P.C.

WESTBOW
PRESS®
A DIVISION OF THOMAS NELSON
& ZONDERVAN

WestBow Press books may be ordered through booksellers or by contacting:

WestBow Press
A Division of Thomas Nelson & Zondervan
1663 Liberty Drive
Bloomington, IN 47403
www.westbowpress.com
844-714-3454

ISBN: 978-1-6642-1812-3 (sc)
ISBN: 978-1-6642-1813-0 (hc)
ISBN: 978-1-6642-1767-6 (e)

Library of Congress Control Number: 2020925865

Print information available on the last page.

WestBow Press rev. date: 01/27/2021

Loving People Well

Linda Bishop Rykowski, M.S., L.C.P.C.

Dedication

To my three sons: Joe, Miles, and Travis. You have been my pride and joy ever since God blessed me with you as my sons! You have enriched my life, and I am very thankful for you!

You went through a lot in your young lives as I dealt with my drug addiction, alcoholism, and then codependency. Even though it affected you greatly, you have risen above it in your adult lives. You are responsible, loving husbands and fathers who I am extremely proud of!

The stronghold of addiction is *not* continuing with you. You have experienced how horrible the consequences are, to individuals and to families.

Now you have married three women who are beautiful, inside and out—Wendy, Jessica, and Darci—and blessed me with eleven wonderful grandchildren: Kaylee, Jesimae, Mikaela, Kaleb, Janelle, Zoey, Jayden, Avery, Brookie, Max, and Ellie.

The cycle of generational strongholds will not persist. God has severed the cords of bondage. Thanks be to God and to each one of you!

Acknowledgments

This book would never have become a reality if it weren't for the help and support of many people. Their names may not be familiar to you but it's important for me to honor them.

First of all, a big thank You to our God! Without Him I would not have finished this book. He kept me going on it and wouldn't let me quit. Even though I stopped writing it many times over the years, He wouldn't let me give up entirely! He knew I just needed more experiences that led to more healing to see the book to completion!

To my three sons, Joe, Miles and Travis Rykowski. Even though I dedicated this book to you I still wanted to thank you and acknowledge you as the greatest gifts God gave me! I wasn't always there for you because of my addictions but you still amaze me every day with your deep passion to be the best person God created you to be! He also granted you beautiful and loving wives, Wendy, Jessica and Darci, to help you to be the best you can be each and every day, and still love you when you can't. I am so thankful for all of you for your love and support, and for gifting me with eleven wonderful grandchildren!

My "adopted daughter," Savannah March, I am grateful that God saw fit to bring us together. From the day you were born, your inquisitive nature endured you to my heart! Now your desire to understand God's love for you and for the whole world has been an adventure to be part of with you! Your understanding and acceptance of Truth encouraged and challenged me to keep growing in my own faith journey. Keep asking questions!

My eleven grandchildren: Kaylee, Jesimae, Mikaela, Kaleb, Janelle, Zoey, Jayden, Avery, Brookie, Max, and Ellie. You make me want to be the beat person I can be, with God's help, so I can be the best grandma I can be so I can help you to be all that God wants you to be! He has a special plan for each one of you, as He tells us in Jeremiah 29:11. I am excited to see what that is for each one of you! I love you so, so much!

My Dad and Mom and thirteen siblings and their spouses, being raised in a family of 14 kids isn't easy. There was plenty of opportunity to learn what works and what doesn't in relationships, but we survived together! I appreciate all of your love, care and support that helped me to make it through life. It's true that you can choose your friends, but you can't choose your family. But if I could, I would still choose you! Each of you has contributed to my life in a special way. Heaven will be so much richer because we will be together for eternity!

My many numerous nieces and nephews, (Yes, Doug, you are counted as one of them. LOL), you made life fun! Even though I got to know some of you better than others because of geographical challenges, I am still grateful to God for bringing all of you into the realm of family! I think of you often and pray for you to carry on the beacon of faith and love of family that you learned from your parents and grandparents, and from others who God knew you needed and would benefit from. Carry on in your own unique ways!

Twelve Step Friends and Sponsors, I am thankful for all of you but because of anonymity I cannot name you specifically, but you know who you are, right? You have helped me learn more and more about addictions and how to overcome them. The recovery journey wasn't meant to travel alone. Thank God He chose all of you to help me in mine! For this I am eternally grateful!

Clients, again because of confidentiality, I cannot name you but I want you to know that without you I wouldn't have worked as hard as I did on my own issues! It was important for me to be as emotionally, mentally, and spiritually healthy as I could be, for your sake as well as mine! Also, I want you to know that sometimes you taught me more than you will ever know! I still think of you and pray that you will continue on your healing journey. We are never finished growing and learning, right?

My friends over the years, again there are too many to name, but each of you played a role in my life at different seasons and for God's specific purposes. I am forever grateful! My most loyal friend, Trista Jackson, I am thankful for all the times we have been able to talk and hang out and laugh together. Your faithful friendship has gotten me through some of my toughest times! Your unfailing love and support have been an example of God's faithfulness to me! You hold a special place in my heart.

Colleagues, Dr. Phil House, Lynn and Lee Oldenberg, Becky Fallon, and Shelley Robbins, who I shared a waiting room with, and Verna Glassing down the hall, you proved invaluable as colleagues, and over time, as trusted friends. I could always count on your wisdom and knowledge in both my professional life and my personal life. I will be forever grateful to God for having our path's cross in this world and I look forward to visiting more in the next! ☺

Preachers, Teachers, and Counselors, you are so numerous, but to name a few, Father Charlie Gorman, Max Soft, Pastor Eric Hutch, Pastor Vern Streeter, Diana Shay, Pastor Tim Weidlich, Pastor Dave Morales, Pastor Nate Poetzl, Pastor

Steve Poetzl, Terri Helmer, Cammie Bergstrom, Diana Krumm, and Ed Smith. Without you I believe my healing and spiritual growth would have stagnated! Thank you for being faithful stewards of His kingdom work!

Last, but definitely not least, to my husband, Ron Rykowski. Your forgiveness and grace constantly remind me of God's continual support, encouragement, and mercy. Your love for me over our many years together, and even when we were apart, amazed me and gave me the confidence to finish writing this book! Thanks for sticking with me through all the craziness! I love you! Let's continue to finish strong together!

Contents

PROLOGUE

Dear Younger Me,

If I knew then what I know now, I wouldn't have done the things I have done.

I wouldn't have made the choices I made.

And I wouldn't have the regrets I do.

But I also wouldn't know now what I didn't know then.

And I wouldn't know God's love!

His is the victory!

Dear Younger Me,

You didn't know how severe the effects of your addictions were.

You didn't know how they affect you and others.

You didn't know that they had the power to destroy you ... and others.

Dear Younger Me,

You didn't know that one day you would be sitting here alone because of it.

You didn't know that it would strip away your understanding of what love is.

You didn't know that it had the power to destroy your self-esteem, your self-image, your "self."

Dear Younger Me,

You didn't even know that you suffered from this awful "dis-ease," and that it would work hard to destroy you.

Dear Younger Me,

When you were twenty-eight, you went to treatment for alcohol and drug dependency.

But, dear younger me, you didn't know that codependency and relationship addiction were also addictions that were destroying you and others.

You didn't know that even before you were born, you were being set up to develop these addictions.

This is my story, but it's really more of a story about God's precious love, mercy, and grace for me and for all of us. I hope that you find some healing and hope. I hope you truly learn to believe that He never leaves us, no matter what we choose to do, even when we are in the worst of what life hands us. For He can restore and redeem all that is lost. His is the victory!

1

REALIZING THE ORIGINS

Wait! God, You formed me this way! You allowed me to be born with an addictive gene! Why? Many reasons, but the main one? Maybe so I would be drawn closer and closer to You? Maybe You knew that it was the only way to get my attention? Maybe I wouldn't need You as much if I didn't have addictions? Maybe I wouldn't be so needy for You?

I've tried to rely on myself and others instead. It doesn't work. It's very painful. I couldn't get in their lifeboat, or if I did, it never took long for me to be cast out again. Left to drown. *If You Want to Walk on Water, You've Got to Get Out of the Boat.* The title of that book by John Ortberg makes even more sense now. I had been desperately trying to get on and stay on other people's lifeboats, but I don't want to play that self-defeating and destructive game anymore. I want to forgive them and myself and move on. But I don't want to try to get on another lifeboat. I can't do that to myself anymore.

If we truly learn the hard lesson of how much You love us, learn to love You back, and then learn to love ourselves in a healthy manner, we won't need others so much. Too much. We won't sin to get their love and acceptance. We won't give up ourselves, who You created us to be. And we won't fall apart so completely when we are once again thrust off the lifeboat.

Donald Miller describes this craziness in his book, *Searching for God Knows What*. God, You *do* know what: love and acceptance. But it first has to come from us believing we are already loved and accepted by You, and then love and accept ourselves. Miller says:

> I kept thinking about all this and I wanted it all to end. I didn't want to be a part of it anymore. Paul kept writing in his books about how people shouldn't want to be circumcised anymore, about how people shouldn't think they were better than other people, about how folks should be submitted to one another in love, thinking of each other as more important than themselves, and I know now, and I realized back in Oakland, that this kind of life could take place only within a relationship with God, the One who takes care of our needs, the One who really has the power to tell us who we are, if we would only trust in Him. (Miller, p. 176)

Wow! Imagine how the world would be if we all lived that way? Imagine how my life would be if I lived that way? One human spirit submitted in love with another human spirit submitted in love? But I don't think it is ever neutral. We all have a sin nature that competes for first place most of the time. We all have a motive. It's a struggle. It's how we are knit in our mother's womb.

Sin nature. An interesting concept. I have often said that I am my worst enemy, and I have helped others to try to understand that about themselves also. We continually make poor choices because of it. We continually hurt ourselves and others because of it. But what if we were submitted to each other in love instead?

The desire to get in the lifeboat with others is destructive to us because it's not really a lifeboat. It is an anchor that will sink us. We have to give up a part of ourselves in order to fit in and be accepted. And if we aren't, then we can become bitter and resentful.

This is exactly what happened to me! I kept trying and trying and trying to get in the lifeboat—to be accepted by them, whoever the "them" was at the time, instead of living in the truth that I was already accepted by my Creator. He didn't want me to get in the lifeboat because it wasn't His will for me. He knew it would destroy me. I thought if I wasn't accepted by them, whoever was in the lifeboat at the time, I was worthless. But He is helping me see this truth more and more. Not just see it, but live it. He helped me learn that my worth is not determined by the them in my life. My worth is not earned. It just is. Because He said so. Period. End of story. And because this is true, I can learn to accept myself.

It's taken me a lifetime to slowly believe this. I threw myself into whatever form of performing I had to do in order to try to get accepted onto the lifeboat, but it was useless and unfulfilling; worse, it was betrayal of myself. I performed at all the different churches I have been to.

But as I contemplate this truth, I realize that this started in my childhood. In my family of origin when I was growing up, I tried hard to have a position in the crazy world of a large family that struggled with addictions. I took on the roles of rescuer and surrogate mother. This developed into codependency.

I also tried to be accepted in the extended family, but because of the different religions, my aunts and uncles and cousins seemed to treat me as though I was less than. It seemed as if they had a holier than thou attitude because of their religious beliefs; as though I was going to go to hell. My mother experienced the same thing until one day she had to assert herself and say to her mother-in-law, my paternal grandmother, that if they could not refrain from talking about religion, then she would not be visiting anymore. As I think about this, I feel sad for her, for them, for us. They didn't know any better. It's what they were taught. But it set me up. Since I never felt accepted by them, my own family members, unless I performed the same way they did, on the lifeboat, I never felt secure in who I was. This put a whole different spin on salvation.

To be fair, I am not sure anything was ever said directly to me about this. But my cousins knew my grandpa and grandma much better than I did. They had a relationship with them that was more than superficial. They belonged to the same church, so they saw each other at least twice a week, on Wednesdays and Sundays. They had each other over for meals, celebrated birthdays and holidays together, and played games together. Now, maybe it's also because there were fourteen of us kids, and only five or seven of them. I don't really know for sure. I just knew that I didn't feel accepted, and I believed it was because of how we chose to practice our faith.

Then I started school and tried hard to be accepted there, but I was too poor, too quiet, and too scared, which was interpreted as me being stuck up. I was different. *Different*— such an interesting word. *Unique* is much better. *Weird* hurts. It's bad to be weird. We all know that.

When do children first perceive that? When do they first experience shame because of it? When is a child first able to discern when he or she is being made fun of, laughed at? One year? Two? By three, for sure!

For example, Mom tells a friend or another family member about something cute he has done in ignorance, and they look at him and laugh, and he feels shame. They aren't really laughing at him, but he is too little to understand, so he feels shame, and he feels the pain. He might not understand it, but he feels it. By five, a child becomes even more aware and will avoid embarrassment at any cost. So by the time a child is school age, he has already experienced being laughed at for his performance and has experienced shame, and will work hard to never feel it again. That is sad. It stunts us from becoming all that God designed us to be and do.

How a child responds to it can make a difference for the rest of his life. Some children decide to be the class clown; making others laugh becomes his worth. The lifeboat, he's been allowed in. But then he has to keep it up. How can he ever be serious? When would anyone ever take him seriously?

Or what if a little girl is sexually abused starting at the age of five? She feels shame, and she takes on her abuser's shame. What happens to her soul? What happens to her identity? Does she just exist for another's pleasure? Is that her lifeboat? It was mine.

Questions for Reflection or Small Group Discussion

1. What lifeboat have you been on or tried to get on?

2. Was it/is it fulfilling or disappointing?

3. What did you/are you learning about yourself?

2

MY RECOVERY STORY

I was born on August 12, 1954, in a small town in Eastern Montana. As the saying goes, my parents tried their best, but with fourteen children to provide food, shelter, and clothing for, there was little time to take care of our emotional needs as well. So as the third oldest, I took on the role of a third parent to most of my siblings, but at the expense of my own nurturing. The pattern was set. I became a controller and rescuer, a "codependent" as it is termed now, forever trying to find someone to meet my needs. This was my identity, and over time it contributed to my many other addictions.

By the time I entered Catholic elementary school at the age of six, I had already learned how to be a chameleon, always trying to make others happy and meeting their needs and desires, as well as following the rules in order to get my needs met until … well, until I didn't. But I will get to that later.

The rules were many, both at home and at school. The priests, the nuns, and the lay teachers were frightening and strict, so being a chameleon helped me survive! Most of them treated me pretty well as long as I obeyed them, including a priest who singled me out for "extra special attention." I had learned to please others to survive, so this seemed no different than when a family member began sexually abusing me at five years of age. He seemed pleased with me afterwards and even rewarded me with special treats, that I just continued doing what he wanted in order to survive and to meet my need for love and acceptance.

He was abusing others as well, which I didn't find out about until years later. It set me up for my own acting out with other children. We had all been abused in one way or another, as we continued to mature.

But when I was twelve years old I decided that I was no longer willing to participate in the sexual acting out. I don't remember exactly what happened to make me decide this, but it may have had something to do with maturing and starting my menstrual cycles and learning more about sex. Or maybe it was a film my class was shown at school about sex. But for whatever reason, I was relieved to stop. I knew it was wrong and carried a great deal of shame around with me concerning it. But unfortunately, the sexual abuse from others went on for many more years.

When I began dating at the young age of thirteen, I

somehow resisted all sexual advances from every boyfriend I ever had, until one in particular. Then I allowed heavy petting but nothing more, until I met my soon-to-be husband.

I was fifteen; he was nineteen. I fell in love with him at first sight, which I now believe was just infatuation because he was home on leave from the Navy. Being a small town teenage girl, I thought he was pretty worldly and exciting. I still wouldn't allow any sex, but when his leave was over and he went back to Rhode Island, we wrote many love letters back and forth, and he called whenever he could, until he was released from the Navy.

By the time he was released, I believed I was truly in love and wanted to spend the rest of my life with him. So I became pregnant at sixteen. We got married two days after I turned seventeen in a hastily thrown-together wedding at the catholic church, after my parents got papers signed by a judge because I was a minor. All I ever wanted was to be loved by someone, have children, and be a stay-at-home mom. I believed I was ready for marriage since I had been a second mom to my younger brothers and sisters for years.

But of course I was too young! That's a huge understatement. As I look back at it now, I realize I just wanted what most humans want—to be loved and accepted just the way I was, unconditionally, and to know and be known completely. Unfortunately, I did not realize this was a hole in my soul, which could only be filled with a relationship with God. I didn't learn that until years later—years after making many bad, destructive decisions.

So there I was, seventeen years old and newly married with a baby on the way. But instead of filling that hole, I was very lonely instead. I came into the marriage with a lot of baggage.

Alcohol and cocaine became my main drugs of choice to run from the pain and myself and my new spouse. By the time I sobered up from them in 1982, at twenty-eight, after going to treatment for five weeks, I had cheated on my husband numerous times. I had tried to fill the hole in my soul with other men, as well as with the alcohol and drugs. But it didn't work.

After treatment, I still hadn't quite accepted this and began using again after four months of sobriety, for four months. But then I quit for good. I cried out to God the morning of my last drunk, and He knew I meant it! He took the desire away immediately. Some call it a spiritual experience. That is how it felt. I joined Alcoholics Anonymous for about seven years and got very active in my church. I did pretty well at staying sober, but I began using busy work as my new drug of choice.

My sons were ten, five, and two years old when I sobered up. I began homeschooling the two older ones the next year, just one year after going to treatment. I felt that we had a lot of lost time to make up for as a family, so I believed this was a good decision. I had a lot of support around me, so it went pretty well. I continued to homeschool for sixteen years.

But besides homeschooling, I dove deeper into church work and other activities. I began teaching Sunday school classes, became an officer in the women's church group, created and organized a carnival at the church, became president of the local and then the state antiabortion groups and lobbied at the state capital for them. I taught marriage classes, along with my husband, at weekend retreats for engaged couples and became the district coordinators for the organization.

I learned to cook and eat all natural foods, grew a garden, and learned to can all kinds of fruits and vegetables. I read through the Bible in a year, recited memorized prayers every day, and attended church three times a week. I began walking three to five miles a day, took in childcare, took in two different nieces at two different times, and homeschooled them too. I hosted the majority of the family holiday celebrations too. I started college in 1995 to earn a bachelor's and then a master's degree in mental health counseling. I could go on, but the point is I was now a very active workaholic.

I was still running from myself and from God. My soul hole did not get filled with all these activities, and I continued to look for someone or something to fill it. This led me to counseling. I started attending counseling sessions in December 1990, eight years after I quit using alcohol and drugs, because although I was accomplishing a lot of things, my marriage was not good, my work addiction had taken over, and I still felt very empty inside. All the busy work allowed me to keep running and keep burying all the pain. But my hurts, habits, and hang-ups didn't dissolve by staying busy. They grew instead.

So besides being a workaholic, I was still acting out another addiction, codependency addiction or relationship addiction, which I later discovered was being driven by *limerence.* (Albert Wakin, an expert on limerence and a professor of psychology at Sacred Heart University, defines limerence as a combination of obsessive-compulsive disorder and addiction—a state of "compulsory longing for another person"; see https://ocdtalk. wordpress.com/tag/albert-wakin/.) So I was always looking for someone I could attach to who I believed was stronger and more self-assured than I was, but who also needed me and needed rescuing, because that's what I was good at doing: rescuing people, usually at my expense, the same thing I did as a child.

Since I was a religious nut by this time, I didn't act out sexually. Still, I had many emotional affairs with men and women in my life, including a professor, a counselor, a legislator, and female friends who I allowed to run my life and mold me into their liking but whom I also tried to control to get my emotional needs met.

In 1990, one friend even insisted, very aggressively and disrespectfully, that I didn't need to attend AA meetings forever, so I quit. That's one symptom of codependency or relationship addiction, or Limerence, doing whatever the other person wants so they won't leave me but rather approve of me and think that I agree with them, at least on the outside. But inside, I became more and more reduced to nothing except sadness, anger, fear, and depression. I would eventually lose my own identity in the other person, trying to be whatever they needed me to be.

But I do need to stop here and say that this was not as black-and-white as it sounds. I would still try to control and fight my way to being separate from them, and this eventually ended friendships because I was so good at choosing a self-focused, narcissistic person, so the relationship was mostly focused on their needs. This was always painful in the end for both of us, but how could it ever really work out as long as I was living out my need to be loved unconditionally and losing myself in the process, leaving God out of the picture?

My marriage continued to deteriorate because I was anything but a faithful wife, especially emotionally. But being his wife, and wanting our marriage to work, I needed him to meet my emotional needs, so I would be okay, so I kept trying to help him be what I needed him to be.

But of course, it didn't work, and so, after thirty-seven years of marriage, I left him in 2008. But as I stepped out of this craziness, I entered into even more dependent relationships.

To quote a classic book, "It was the best of times. It was

the worst of times." It was the worst of times because my addictions and codependency would climb to a new height of insanity. But it was the best of times because I would receive more healing than I ever thought I needed or was possible and a deep relationship with Jesus that I had always wanted.

The unhealthy emotional dependence took on a life of its own. I had become enmeshed with others, and once again I gave my identity away. I even quit my counseling practice for a while. This was mainly due to my husband and I selling our house because of the divorce; my counseling office was in our house.

I even gave up precious time with my grandkids and sons, so I could be available to others. I gave up my likes and dislikes and replaced them with others. Remember, I had learned to be a chameleon at a very young age, and it is one of the symptoms of relationship addiction. Over time, I perfected this, apparently, losing almost all sense of my own identity.

QUESTIONS FOR REFLECTION OR SMALL GROUP DISCUSSION

1. What is your story?

2. What mile markers had the most influence on you, for good or bad?

3. What choices did you make, positive or negative, because of them?

3

THE BEGINNING OF THE END

Something I did not see coming was how much of my true self I would lose. I was desperate to not lose others' acceptance, so I did whatever it took to keep it, but in the end, I lost both their acceptance and my own self-respect.

In Genesis, when Cain killed his brother, Abel, it was because of jealousy over Abel's sacrifice being more acceptable by God, because God knew Cain's heart wasn't in it for the right reason. He was trying to earn God's acceptance his own way. He didn't realize he already had it. So he tried to compete with his brother instead and make God love him. He tried to be secure under his own power. I did the same thing in my relationships.

Satan hasn't changed his tactics. He still tempts us to be secure in ourselves—in how we look, what we do, who we know, what we have. I call this the three P's: Pride, Position, and Purse (money and things). But it doesn't work. We still remain like Cain. He wanted God's acceptance but wasn't willing to give up his own idea on how to get it. His faith was in himself, instead of in God's endless love for him. His punishment for killing his brother was to be a wanderer, forever seeking after satisfaction while being laden down with guilt.

That is how I lived most of my life. I kept seeking after satisfaction in approval from people, aside from God, but it didn't work. It never does. It may appear to for a while, but it always ends up disappointing us. We also usually end up getting hurt and hurting others.

We were designed to attach first to our parents or caregivers, who are supposed to lead us to attach to God in healthy ways, but if this doesn't happen, we have "a deep black hole within that cries for love and acceptance" (Fernee, p. 139). We all use something or someone to try to fill that black hole. Wounded people wound people. It was only by the grace of God that we survived this craziness.

I slowly began to realize how bizarre my behavior had become, and God directed me to a path of healing. I began expressing my own opinions and likes and dislikes again, but things went from bad to worse for a while, since I was still caught in my codependency. I continued to give in sometimes, and others believed that I agreed with them and that I was the one who was wrong and needed to change. I continued to take responsibility for almost every argument and promised to change so others would be okay and not be angry with me anymore, just loving and accepting me instead.

My self-esteem was pretty much shot by this time, and the shame caused me to isolate, so I believed I had no one to go to who could help me out of this insanity, no one who would understand the depth of the pain I kept exposing myself to and the all-encompassing codependent addiction.

I became more and more angry with myself, and I desperately wanted to be set free, but I still couldn't break free of the bondage on my own. After trying everything in my own power, I finally cried out to God again. I was on my hands and knees in my bedroom after yet another disagreement with a friend in which I took the blame. But this time I really surrendered, begging God to release me from the bondage to this addiction.

Unlike when I cried out to God to set me free from my bondage to drugs and alcohol, He did not release me right away. He knew I was not ready to give up some of my unhealthy friendship behavior entirely and walk away, so I remained caught in my bondage a little longer, continuing to take the blame for every problem in my relationships.

When I was ready to quit drugs and alcohol, I cried out to God that I didn't want to do them anymore. He knew I was ready and took the desire away immediately, instantaneously. I have never used drugs or alcohol since November 14, 1982, except for a two-month experiment in 2005 when I tried drinking wine just on social occasions. It didn't work, of course, and I got back on the recovery path quickly.

But this drug—this addiction—was different. I was trying to quit the codependent addiction without giving up my unhealthy ways of interacting. God had to show me that the desire for my friendships was like being in relationship with my drugs. It was like trying not to drink or use drugs but keeping them available to myself. It wasn't possible.

Through my healing journey, I compared it to swimming in a big vat of whiskey, trying to stay afloat but not being a good swimmer. Not having a lifejacket, I kept going under. I couldn't climb out, and there was nothing to hold on to. I needed to be rescued! I couldn't save myself. Thank God, Jesus agreed, and He didn't give up on me! He kept throwing me a life jacket of one kind or another.

One life preserver came by way of a book called *No Stones*. The author, Marnie Fernee, was a sex and relationship addict and had opened a treatment facility called Bethesda Workshop in Nashville, Tennessee, to help those like myself who were caught in relationship addiction. I called the number on the back of the book and signed up to attend in January 2014, but even before I left, Jesus sent me another life preserver.

I attended church on January 12, 2014, and heard a sermon that went straight to my heart. It was about living life without regrets. I came home from church that day and made the decision to move out on my own and live alone for a while. I had been renting an apartment with a friend since I had left my husband. I had never lived alone before, and I was scared, but I was also very excited.

I knew Jesus was releasing me from the stranglehold of my relationship/codependency addiction, so without much argument with Him, for once, I trusted Him and began looking for a place.

God, being God, found me a place to buy just four days later. I made an offer on it the next day, and it was accepted. I felt as if I had climbed out of the vat of whiskey. But I realized that my struggle was still going to be hard, and it was.

Some days, I didn't just climb back in the vat. I dove in headfirst. At these times, I felt out of control, like a recovering alcoholic running into a bar recklessly, believing she could have just one quick drink and then leave, feeling better. Instead of feeling better, I felt defeated and like a harlot. I was running after people instead of God to meet my need for acceptance. I would get so angry and depressed afterward that I would isolate even more. I recognized that because of my addiction, I still felt like I was less than others and that, around them, I still had very little worth.

So I continued to flounder, continually trying to get my emotional needs, my hole in my soul, met in unhealthy ways. But I knew. I knew I was still acting out my addiction and I needed to stop. So finally I hit my knees again, begging Him to save me from myself. I surrendered. I cried out to Him that, again, just the way it had been with alcohol and drugs, I didn't want to do it anymore. It was still a slow process, but He helped me more and more to resist the temptation to run after my drug of choice.

I continued to attend Alcoholics Anonymous, as well as Al-Anon, but it wasn't working very well, even though I had a sponsor and was working the steps. I knew I needed more. Growing up catholic, I had a pretty good understanding of and belief in God, but I didn't understand the whole relationship with Jesus thing. I knew He had died for my sins and, therefore, because I believed it, that I was going to heaven when I died, but I hadn't been too willing to allow Him to get very close to me. After all, he was part human, and I had been hurt by many humans in my life, as I'm sure all of us have.

But I knew I needed to surrender completely and give up *all control*, which, up to this time, I had not been willing to do. I have a saying taped on my refrigerator about this: "Show me a man with an addiction, and I'll show you a man who demands reliable pleasure and is angry with an unmanageable God." How accurate is that when it comes to us addicts?

I was also hesitant to come to Him because, after all, He knew all the stupid, crazy things I had done and how much I had pursued others, instead of Him, to try to feel loved and worthy, so He was probably not very happy with me. Also, as crazy as it sounds, I figured He must not be very strong because He let others mistreat Him and kill Him. In my addictive mind, I needed someone strong—someone who could take care of me and love me, no matter what. I hadn't fully grasped that climbing onto the cross was a choice He made to save me and to save all of us, as only the living God could do!

But I became willing to explore the idea of surrendering to Him and allowing Him to lead me in all areas of my life. I really wanted a deep, personal relationship with Him even though I was scared of it at the same time, so I decided that I would search for a Christ-centered twelve-step recovery group. Maybe then I could finally grab hold of a relationship with Jesus and move ahead in my healing.

God led me to Hope Center where I began attending Celebrate Recovery (CR), but after I attended my second Women's Alcohol and Chemical Dependency Group, I realized that I really needed a group that was more specific to my addiction for approval. So out of desperation, I asked Pastor Ben, the lead pastor of Hope Center, if we could start one. He and his wife, Jodi, willingly listened to my story and supported the idea, if I would lead it. I felt humbled by the offer but accepted—as long as they would help me, to make sure I followed all the guidelines of CR since I was relatively new to it.

Ben and Jodi heard and understood and yet still accepted me, despite my openness and honesty about this awful addiction and the things I had done. I will be eternally grateful to both Ben and Jodi!

That was in September 2015, and my relationship with Jesus *is* deeper and stronger than it has ever been, and it continues to grow. Ben and Jodi listened, they heard, and they responded, so here I am telling you my story in the hopes that it will help anyone who is suffering from this destructive and all-consuming addiction.

As the new contemporary Christian song goes, "The cross made me flawless," so even though in our human economy the sins I committed, while actively engaged in my addictions, should have qualified me for hell, and disqualified me for being of any use to God or anyone else, there I was at CR serving Him instead. That's how God's economy works. He takes our awful addictions and makes beauty out of ashes.

Also, as part of my healing journey, on November 14, 2015, the day I celebrated thirty-three years of sobriety from alcohol and drugs, I talked with my former husband and confessed what I had done in my relationship/codependency addiction, while I was still married to him, and to ask for his forgiveness. I had hurt him a lot in our thirty-seven years of marriage, so he couldn't forgive quite yet, but since that time he has been willing to attend family events that I am at and even socializes with me. In fact, we even exchange gifts at Christmas. God is good, and I know now that He truly does redeem and restore, and He will continue to do so!

After I talked with my former husband that day, I also went to each of our three sons to confess to them and to ask for forgiveness too. When I had been active in my codependency/relationship addiction and left their father because of it, I pretty much abandoned them. Even though they were married and had kids of their own by this time, I had gone from being the matriarch of the family—the one who hosted almost all of our celebrations including Christmas, Thanksgiving, Easter, and some of the birthday parties—and had also abandoned their children by not being available to them as a loving grandma should be. I had been spending very little time with them and even excluded them from my hiking and camping trips, going to movies, going to the park to play Folf (Frisbee golf), vacation trips, and a host of other activities because I was caught in my addiction.

My sons and their wives forgave me immediately, but I will never forget my youngest son's words. He said, "I would like to think that this is a sin that only affected you, Mom, but unfortunately it's not. It hurt all of us." This is the same son who told me, on my thirtieth sobriety birthday in 2012, that my sobriety from alcohol and drugs is what changed my sons' lives for the better when they were growing up. I will never forget those words either, because although I would like to believe that I suffered the consequences of my addictions alone, I did not. Our addictions affect all those around us, but so does our sobriety, so there was no better way to celebrate my sobriety birthday, from alcohol and drugs, then to ask them for forgiveness for this latest addiction of mine and continue the healing journey together.

I went to bed that night feeling freer than ever before, and more determined than ever before to never get caught in this addiction or any of my other addictions again, with God's help. I had taken steps eight and nine with those who I had hurt the most, and I had come out the other side.

After this, I continued to make amends with others I had hurt, including my friends and other family members, and with the help of God and accountability partners, I will continue to do so, as He leads me. Each time I do, I feel more and more peace—a peace that is beyond all understanding.

Recovery programs work! Jesus works! And I will continue to serve Him, and I know He will continue to heal me as I go, because that's how He works. What Scripture tells us is true: "Therefore, if anyone is in Christ, he is a new creation, the old has gone, the new has come!" (2 Corinthians 5:17 NIV 1984) I wrote a poem a few years ago about this.

JESUS IS THE REASON

I don't get it,
I probably never will.
I've made mistakes many times;
I deserve hell.

But the more I mess up,
The more He forgives me.
He lifts me up
And once again says, "Follow Me."

Love others well,
But I hurt others a lot.
I'll never get it perfect,
But about that, it's not.

It's not about me,
It's not about the "must,"
It's not about performing;
It's about Trust.

But I built walls to keep others out.
Trust was too risky and hard.
He knew I had been hurt
And was scared and on guard

But together we can do it;

He can be my guide.

Love is worth it;

That is why He died.

So I let down my walls;

I let go of fear and blame.

I began to trust again

And to even let go of shame.

I quit hiding;

I let others get close.

His love for me is the reason,

For every grace-filled season of growth!

QUESTIONS FOR REFLECTION OR SMALL GROUP DISCUSSION

1. Have you been in an addictive relationship? If so, how did it affect you?

2. How did you escape? What life preservers did God send you?

3. Are you able to let down the walls that keep others out, and you trapped inside, with God's guidance? If not, what is keeping you from allowing Him to direct your path of healing?

4

AN AWAKENING

So where did all this addiction come from? How did I get so unhealthy? Well, since I'm a counselor I am of course going to say it started in my childhood. But let me take that apart a bit.

As I revealed in the first chapter, I was the third oldest of fourteen, and I took on the role of caregiver in the family fairly early. In doing so, I did not get my own needs met, but even more than that, I came to believe that my needs were not important. I was not important. I learned much later in life that this is referred to as emotional abandonment.

But as I matured, I worked hard at trying to be important. I wanted to be approved of very badly, but I didn't want anyone to know that I needed that. Hersh, in *The Last Addiction* (2008), writes that even though an addict wants approval, we don't want others to know that we do. So we act very self-sufficient and self-confident and won't let others get close enough for us to develop an intimate bond with them. But underneath, that is all we really want.

Joyce Meyer wrote a book entitled *Approval Addiction* (2005). She says:

> Those who have been hurt badly through abuse or severe rejection, as I have, often seek approval of others to try to overcome their feelings of rejection and low self-esteem … they suffer from these feelings and use the addiction of approval to try to remove the pain. They are miserable if anyone seems to not approve of them in any way or for any reason and they are anxious about the disapproval until they are once again accepted. They may do almost anything to gain the approval they feel they have lost—even things their conscience tells them are wrong. (Meyer, p. vii)

After I bought my own place and was living alone for the first time, I began to try to put the pieces of my life, of me, back together. I did everything I could to find answers to what I had been through over the last five years. I began seeking out support and healthier friendships. I went to counselors to try to make more sense of what I had gone through and to grow from it. I continued to attend twelve-step programs and work the steps with the help of sponsors and accountability partners too.

I was determined to learn all I could about this addiction and how and why it had taken a stranglehold on me. I knew that in order to be free of it, I had to understand it. After all, knowledge is powerful, and we can't fight what we don't understand.

During my healing process, I struggled with some memories concerning my mother, but when she passed away in 2009, I wrote this memory about her because although we didn't always see eye to eye, I still loved her and knew that I would miss her. Also, I know she'd done her very best as a mom, the same way I did. I made mistakes too, plenty of them! My sons can attest to that. We all do, so I do not judge her. Besides, she also had a ton of good qualities too.

Linda Rykowski, M.S., L.C.P.C.

Her Last Hours

As she lay there fading away from us, we often wondered, sometimes to ourselves, "Is she still breathing?" The hospital bed in the living room was partially reclined; the crisp white sheets were crisp no longer. The numerous medicine bottles sat upon the bedside table, reminding all of us that our mother was no longer the bass playing, oil painting, *Gunsmoke* watching, enthusiastic woman we knew.

There would be no more calls from her telling us of the next family reunion or camping trip. No more card playing or halloopsee making. As we sat in silence and waited for her spirit to be taken … these thoughts and more made us both smile and weep.

Dad anxiously hovered around her, like the hummingbirds outside her window … devoted husband for fifty-nine years. He had aged over the last six months as he watched his faithful mate slip away. His hair was streaked with more snow than before, his shoulders slumped over as if he were carrying a great weight, and the sparkle in his eyes had dimmed.

Finally, her last breath was breathed. We were released from the waiting but not the loss. As we prepared for her funeral, we had many opportunities to share our grief with each other, as we had one week earlier when our sister had died from the same evil. Now we had two loved ones gone from us.

As we walked away from the second funeral in ten days, we were quiet, lost in our thoughts. And we went our separate ways.

Questions for Reflection or Small Group Discussion

1. What was your awakening? Or what awakening do you need?

2. What have you done to move in the right direction?

3. Did you draw closer to God through it?

5

THE PROCESS OF FORGIVING

It is sad when a sin's effect is generational. We all learn to cope one way or another. Trying to outrun the fear and shame is pretty common. I soon learned that my addiction functioned like most addictions: it was a way to run from myself and from Jesus. So as I have already shared, I started attending a Christ-centered twelve-step program in hopes that I could develop my relationship with Him. Up to this time, I had gone through quite a few years of trying to do this relationship my way. But it wasn't working. Crazy as it sounds, I really separated out God the Father from Jesus, His Son. I didn't have a problem submitting to God the Father, but up until this time, I was *not* going to submit to a person who could potentially hurt me. I really did not understand Jesus and His role in my life.

But Jesus met me right where I was. He didn't force Himself on me. He beckoned to me but not in a harsh, demanding way. He was so gentle about it that I wasn't really aware of when I actually began to love Him and accept His love for me. So as I grew in my understanding of my addiction, I also grew in my understanding of Him.

He began helping me ask some pretty intense questions. What had driven me to stay in the relationship addiction for so long? Why hadn't I stood up for myself more and stopped accepting abuse sooner? Why did I keep trying to fix broken or unhealthy relationships that were beyond repair? Why did I keep taking the blame? As Jesus helped me answer these questions and others, my anger grew. I soon learned that if I didn't get a handle on it, it was going to destroy me. I had already done many things out of anger. I wanted to quit.

Jesus helped me realize that what was holding me back the most was an inability to forgive myself and others, which caused me to lack self-love and self-care and fed a deep, dark need to blame others. So I was caught.

But in recovery from this awful "dis-ease," I learned that forgiveness of myself and others was the only way to true healing. Sometimes, I still wrestled with myself first and tried to hold on to my self-righteousness and my hurt and anger at those who had hurt me. But when I would get humble and become willing to let it go and admit my part, God helped me choose to forgive both myself and the others who were involved.

Jesus tells us in Matthew 5:23–24 (MSG),

This is how I want you to conduct yourself in these matters. If you enter your place of worship and are about to make an offering, you suddenly remember a grudge a friend has against you, abandon your offering, leave immediately, go to this friend and make things right. Then and only then, come back and work things out with God.

In other words, admit your wrongs ... promptly, and forgive. That's pretty clear, huh?

As I was working through forgiving myself and others, I realized that part of the reason I struggled with it was because I had held on to some secrets about some of my biggest regrets. Many of us have been keeping secrets all of our lives. Every day these secrets take a toll on us. The toll we pay is loss of self-respect and an ability to have healthy, open relationships because we are in bondage to them. But admitting those secrets out loud to a trusted friend or family member, or a professional in some cases, strips them of their power. They lose much of their hold on us when they are shared.

Despite this, sometimes we are still afraid to reveal our secrets to another person, even someone we trust. We somehow feel as if we have everything to lose and nothing to gain. While attending Celebrate Recovery, I learned that there are three things we lose and three things we gain by bringing our secrets out into the open and forgiving ourselves and others:

1. **We lose our sense of *isolation*.** This is because someone is going to join us where we are hiding. It is important to share with someone as soon as possible, once we have decided to do this. Our sense of aloneness will begin to vanish. That's a *big* plus!

Personally, I found this to be very true! I shared my fourth and fifth steps the first time when I was in a treatment facility in 1982 for alcohol and drugs. (The fourth and fifth steps of all recovery groups state: 4) "Made a searching and fearless moral inventory of ourselves" and 5) "Admitted to God, to ourselves and to another human being the exact nature of our wrongs.")

The group leaders had us split into small groups to do the fifth step. When it was my turn, I was nervous, but I found that it was a real relief to share all the crazy, stupid things I had done when I was under the influence of alcohol and drugs. After I shared, each member of the group was given the opportunity to give me feedback on what I had shared. A lot of them expressed how they related, and for the first time I didn't feel so alone. I felt understood and accepted. It was awesome!

2. **We will begin to lose our unwillingness to *forgive.***
   When people accept us despite what we have done, we
   start to forgive ourselves too, and then we can begin to
   extend forgiveness to others who have hurt us.

I did another fourth and fifth step in 2013, this time in
regard to my relationship/codependency addiction. As I said
earlier, this addiction had almost destroyed me entirely. It
had left me with very little self-respect and had filled me with
more shame and guilt than I had ever experienced before. I
also realized that I had tons of anger and even rage at times,
some directed at myself. I didn't think I would ever be able
to forgive myself or those who had hurt me. But through the
process of sharing all that had happened as a result of my poor
choices and my addictions, my willingness to forgive others
and myself grew.

I was surprised and grateful when my sponsor, who listened
to all the craziness I had put myself through, still accepted me
after I shared all my secrets and bad decisions. This led me to
be able to let go of the anger and the shame and guilt and the
deep rage that made me want revenge. I wanted to hurt those
who had hurt me, but I was able to release this desire through
the grace of God and His forgiveness toward me.

I didn't deserve forgiveness, but I came to the understanding
that it's not about deserving it. It's about His grace and mercy
for me. With this new understanding, I was able to release

others from all the ways they had hurt me. I'm sure you have heard that forgiving others is a gift that we give ourselves, and not forgiving a person is like drinking poison and hoping the other person will die. The bitterness destroys us. But once we forgive, we are free from this bondage. This certainly was true for me!

3. **We will lose our inflated, false *pride*.** As we see and accept who we are, we begin to gain true humility, which involves seeing ourselves as we really are and seeing God as He really is and who we are in Him.

Through sharing my fourth step, I was able to grow in humility and admit that because of my addiction I had brought on a lot of my own pain. I was responsible for allowing myself to be hurt. I had made many bad choices that led to being abused. I had used pride to cover up my shame and self-loathing. Once my pride was out of God's way, He helped me see this, which led to my next huge step.

4. **We will lose our sense of *denial*.** Being truthful with another person will tear away our denial. We begin to feel clean and honest.

Boy! That's an understatement!

Relationship/codependency addiction is driven by denial and fantasy. I had not been willing to admit and live in reality. But once I began sharing my fourth step, I was able to see how much denial I had been in. Once I began being honest with myself, I was able to admit that I had placed the majority of the blame on others instead of myself. This had made it harder to forgive, but now I could admit my share of the responsibility and forgive myself as well as others. (I'll go into that more later.)

So there we are. Now that I've shared what we have to *lose* when we admit our wrongs to another, I would like to share three benefits we can *gain*.

1. **We gain the *healing*** that the Bible promises. James 5:16 (NIV) says: "Confess your sins to each other and pray for each other so that you may be healed." The key word here is *healed*. The verse doesn't say, "Confess your sins to each other and pray for each other so you will be forgiven." God *forgives* us when we confess our sins to *Him*. But when we confess our sins to one another, He knows we will begin to be free of the shame that holds us back from the healing process.

Let me stress that point again because this is key as to why telling our sins to another is such an important part of our healing process. God forgives us when we confess our sins to Him, but the healing really takes hold when we confess our sins to each other.

When I did my fifth step in 1982 at treatment, and a more thorough one with my first sponsor in 1984, and then later in 2013 with another sponsor, I found this to be very true. Each time I shared, I experienced more and more freedom from the bondage of fear and shame and the hideous self-loathing, and I experienced more and more healing!

2. **We gain *freedom*.** Our secrets have kept us in chains—bound, frozen, unable to move forward in our relationship with God as well as with others. Admitting our sins *snaps* the chains so God's healing power can begin. Psalm 107:13–14 (TLB) reminds us of this: "They cried to the Lord in their troubles, and He rescued them! He led them from the darkness and shadow of death and snapped their chains."

So now, whenever I realize that I am upset with someone or that someone is upset with me, I try to be quick to admit my fault, but because of my relationship/codependency addiction I have to really examine the situation first.

Sometimes an apology is not what is needed. Sometimes the situation calls for more clarification and understanding. We don't want to take responsibility for the wrong reason. Sometimes codependency leads us to take the blame for things that are not our responsibility. We do this for unhealthy reasons—e.g., so the person will still accept us or so we will still feel like we are in control. But that is destructive to both ourselves and the other person. It's a tricky business though, because sometimes our ego gets in the way, and we just want to be right. So when things aren't clear, it's a good idea to talk it over with someone you trust.

I can still hear my Al-Anon sponsor's voice guiding me: "Do you want to be right, or do you want to happy?" I hated it when she first said that years ago when I was going through some of my worst stuff, but now I appreciate those words and heed them. After all, Jesus forgave me and continues to forgive me. When I'm struggling with forgiving someone, I try to remember this. It helps tremendously! It has the power to take my pride and judgmental attitude out of the picture and replaces them with humility so I can be free to forgive.

I wrote this poem to express this:

FREE TO FORGIVE

I've been set free—
Oh, yes, indeed!
Christ carried my cross;
Now He is my Boss!

I suffered greatly when I judged,
But now I know that I finally budged!
I no longer carry anger and shame.
God redeemed me even though I was to blame!

He loves each one of us so much,
Even those who have hurt us and such!
We, too, have sinned and hurt others,
But He forgives us and all our sisters and
brothers!

Now we can live in freedom and love.
That's how His justice works from above!
For when we choose to love instead of hate,
It is what changes our present and our eternal
fate!

Questions for Reflection or Small Group Discussion

1. What, if any, religion did you experience while growing up? How did this affect your self-worth?

2. Who have you needed to forgive? Have you started the process? If so, what have you gained from it? If not, what do you need to do to start the process?

3. What have you needed to forgive yourself for? Have you been able to yet? If so, what did you gain from it? If not, what is in your way?

6

SURRENDER

The Vat: I shared earlier how being caught in my relationship/ codependency addiction was like being caught in a vat of whiskey and not being able to get out, but Jesus sent me two life preservers. The first was information about a treatment facility that I was able to go to; the second was a sermon that gave me the courage to move out of an apartment I was sharing with a friend and to buy my own place.

God recently gave me a new vision of the vat. The big vat of whiskey that I had been drowning in for many years had burst open and turned into water, which was now flowing out into the world, giving life. I believed this to mean that because of the addictions that I suffered, as well as my professional life as a counselor, He was using me to help others get free too, bringing new life and washing away the addiction, the shame, the despair, the loneliness, the low self-esteem, and low self-worth.

I was now able to recognize relationship/codependency addiction and share what I had learned about how to be healed of this awful, destructive bondage.

I couldn't get out of the vat of whiskey on my own. I had taken hold of the lifejackets He threw me, and I wasn't drowning anymore, but I was still just treading water inside the vat. I still tried to control my addiction on my own, but I finally came to believe and accept that I couldn't. Period. That's all. I just couldn't. So I surrendered.

My yearning for connection and acceptance is really about feeling a lack in myself and needing a deep, personal relationship with Jesus. I know that now. My journey to be accepted has been painful because I have tried to meet that yearning with imposters: people, positions, power, belonging, acceptance, connection, to be known, and to know. All of these are part of the human experience, but if they are used as a replacement for a deep, personal relationship with Jesus, they will leave me feeling empty once again and unfulfilled. Nothing satisfies like a relationship with Him.

To get into a relationship with Jesus, I have to accept that I need to let go of control. This can be scary, but when I remember that He loves me no matter what, I'm a bit more willing to jump into His arms and let Him lead me. He loves me unconditionally, which just makes me want to be the best person I can be. Funny how that works!

Step seven in the addiction recovery process is "Humbly

asked Him to remove all my defects of character." So to take my hands off of my life and open them to Jesus, giving Him control, requires that I examine all my faults, admit them to Him, and humbly ask Him to remove them. But first I have to be made aware of them and admit them. That's hard—but oh, so healing! Bill W., the founder of Alcoholics Anonymous, said that "humility is a healer of pain." I believe that to be so; it certainly has been in my life.

Recently, this fact hit me on the head and slammed me to the ground. I had a family member share with me how some of my behavior was upsetting to her and even to a couple of my grandkids. When we met to talk about it, I listened with all my heart because she had made it clear that even though she didn't like some of my behavior, she still loved me. That made it a lot easier to swallow my pride and be willing to hear her and make some changes about myself.

But it still hurt. It hurt a lot! It injured my pride most of all. But it also grieved me into repentance. I began praying and journaling about the things she said. Soon I realized that the only way I was going to be able to move forward and make some necessary changes was to get back into a twelve-step program and find a sponsor or accountability partner. So I did. I also began reading everything I could about the sixth and seventh steps, which deal with getting healed of my defects of character. I brought them before the Lord and asked His help in removing them.

Boy, I'm sure glad that God used a loving family member the way He did. I've said many times that *I am my own worst enemy.* That is more abundantly clear now than ever before. Pride kept me stuck and kept me thinking I could get healed on my own. But it didn't work for me. It took this loving family member to help me realize this once again and continue moving forward.

I wrote a poem about this a few years ago that I'd like to share with you.

Sobriety

Thirty-five years ago today
I began to live a whole new way.
No more alcohol and drugs for me.
Instead, I made the decision to be free!

Free of addiction, fear and pain.
Oh, I had so much to gain.
At times, it's been a long hard road
But a journey with a much lighter load!

Jesus, You have shown me the way.
Life keeps getting better day after day.
Gone are the regrets and shame.
Instead, love, joy and peace came!

I couldn't have done it without Your love.
Many blessings have come from above.
It's not always easy and carefree,
But even then, You are there with me!

So *thank You* for thirty-five years of sobriety!

Questions for Reflection or Small Group Discussion

1. Have you been trapped in a "Vat"? Why?

2. How did you/are you getting set free from it?

3. Who can you thank for it? Who can you pass on the knowledge and wisdom to?

7

HE REDEEMS AND RESTORES

I read somewhere that there are really only two emotions, either fear or love, and that everything that we do or don't do is motivated by one emotion or the other. That fascinates me! To be able to take my hands off of my life, and the way it should go, to lay it all down, even though I feel fear. *Wow!* That's freedom! But it must be because of my love for Him and trust in His love for me. Then it is easy, or easier. Love is the opposite of fear.

I'm reminded that "there are more lifeguards than sharks." I believe it was Donald Miller who wrote that in one of his many books that I have read. That stuck with me because trusting others is something I've struggled with most of my life. I realize now that it's a process. It's slow. It's meant to be.

But relationship/codependency addiction says otherwise. This sickness is so compulsively disgusting and damaging that lives can be forever ruined. I can think of several people who have been hurt tremendously by jumping in too quickly to a relationship and getting hurt beyond what seems bearable. Including me. I know too that we relationship/codependent addicts continue to stay way too long in relationships that are painful and destructive. We keep believing we can fix it if we just keep trying. The need to be loved and accepted has driven me to do this and be hurt over and over again, but I know now that losing can make me better.

I have "lost" many relationships, including some that should never have been. God is making a masterpiece out of the pain. He uses it for my good and His glory. What I have been seeking after turns around and bites me so hard I think I am going to die. But I don't. I go to Him because He knows how to bind up my wounds. And even more, He teaches me through them what true love is—and what it isn't. There are relationships that appear to be real, but they are masquerades of the true thing. Fantasies really.

So why did I stay in these masquerades, playing a part, for so long? Why didn't I leave unhealthy relationships way before I did? What story was I trying to write? Fiction. Was reality so much harder to accept and live out? Pretending it was something, or I could make it something that it was not? A fantasy. But if I had been honest with myself earlier, I could have been free much sooner.

So much hurt. So much pain. So much dysfunction. So many tangled webs. If I could just fix it. If I could just change.

Then I could make it perfect. But it doesn't work that way. The same is true when only one person in a relationship is changing and trying to make it work. It can't work. If the other is busy using the defenses of blaming the other person and trying to shame them into submission, and also staying busy so as to stay out of the relationship, it can't work. So leaving and beginning the long, odious journey of recovery is necessary.

It's funny how sometimes we have to leave a relationship in order to learn how to be healthy in a relationship. When you haven't got another person to focus on, and it's just you looking back at yourself in the mirror, things become much more obvious and even serendipitous. But it can also be peaceful, at times. Learning to love myself was like that.

There was a time I couldn't look myself in the eye when I looked in a mirror. I could do my hair and put on my makeup, but I never really looked at myself. It was a queer sort of feeling to truly stare at myself in the mirror and actually like the person staring back. It was like the first time I ever looked out the window of a plane flying high above the clouds. It feels otherworldly. Or maybe heavenly would fit better. Not that I am heavenly, but the experience itself is. I can imagine at those times when I look at myself that I'm a pretty okay person, someone I wouldn't mind being friends with.

Why did I have to go through all the pain to get there, though? That kind of still boggles my mind. I have an eight-by-eleven-inch picture of myself as about a six or seven-month-old baby sitting up looking scared but curious. That's kind of how it feels looking at myself in the mirror. Sort of like wondering if I am going to allow myself to be hurt again, or if I've learned to stop it before it starts.

Trust. That baby is asking me if she can trust me. She is a reflection of my own image in the mirror. Can I trust me? I am learning. As I do, I find that I have more and more peace because I know now that I don't have to be perfect. I can make mistakes now and laugh instead of beating myself up and feeling shame. It is so freeing to do so! I am teaching my grandkids to do so too. I let them know: "You weren't created to be perfect. You were created to be real." So very true!

So why do we do it? Why do we look to another person to meet all our emotional needs and beat ourselves up when it doesn't work out? Earlier I mentioned a book God sent to me when I was trying to get free of my addictive bondage in a relationship: *No Stones* by Marnie Ferree (2010). She writes about the different kinds of abandonment we can experience in childhood and how it affects us. She addresses four kinds: physical, emotional, sexual, and spiritual. When I took another look at this recently, I realized how much the emotional abandonment caused me to get into a number of unhealthy relationships over the years. She quotes Laaser's (2004) description of emotional abandonment as "no listening, no caring or nurturing, and no expression of affection" (p. 133). No hand reaching out in love.

She also mentions that this can be generational. I've already shared how it affected me, but I realize now that it also affected my parenting. As I shared earlier, I was caught in my alcohol and drug addiction in my son's early years. It hurts my heart to think about it now … but God—God is the Great Healer. I know I can't undo the emotional damage I caused, but I know that God can and has been doing so. As I also shared, all three are amazing fathers and husbands. So the generational damage doesn't have to continue. And neither I, nor they, have to continue making unhealthy emotional bonds. We have a choice. That is good news, indeed!

In all honesty, I don't do this perfectly. But I am a lot quicker at recognizing the pattern and backing off before I get hurt or hurt the other person. I am so grateful for being able to do this now. It saves me a ton of heartache.

Sometimes God uses someone else to help me see it. Like a good friend, for instance. Sometimes she is good at seeing my over-involvement with a person or organization before I am. I am very grateful for her care and insight, and I thank her and God for this protection. As I said earlier, sometimes I am my own worst enemy. But I know it's because of my abandonment issues. They still sneak up and bite me at times. I am grateful that God has put people in my life to help me see it sooner. We truly do need others.

Questions for Reflection or Small Group Discussion

1. Have you learned/are you learning to love yourself in a healthy way?

2. What things do you do, or not do, that show this?

3. What do you think of the statement, "You weren't created to be perfect. You were created to be real"?

8

A Father's Love

Donald Miller wrote a book about fathers and our need for them in *Father Figure*. His ideas resonate with me big-time. I realize I've not had a father figure to rely on consistently. I don't mean any disrespect here. I loved my dad when he was alive, and I still love him in heaven and look forward to seeing him again. I know that he tried his best. My dad worked hard to keep food on the table and clothes on our backs and a roof over our heads. He tried his best to help us through our emotional upheavals of life too.

Take for instance when my best friend in high school was very upset because her family was moving away in the middle of our junior year, and she did not want to go. And I didn't want her to go either! My dad and mom let her live with us to finish out the year. He already had fourteen mouths to feed, but he opened his arms to one more. That's just the kind of guy he was. He helped others whenever he could. He was well known in town for his family of fourteen kiddos, but he was equally well known for his big heart. Everybody liked him! Of course, he made mistakes as a parent. What parent hasn't? I often heard him say that if he had it to do over again he'd change some of his parenting mistakes. I think we all would, right? In fact, once I became an adult, I knew I could go to him anytime I needed help with anything. He had a listening ear and a big heart, and he would even help us out financially if we needed it.

But because of not getting all my emotional needs met consistently while growing up, I continually felt deficient; like I didn't quite measure up. Now, though, I'm learning that God is my Father, and I don't need to struggle with getting and staying in the "lifeboat" anymore. Instead, He rescued me from it. It wasn't safe anyway with all the turbulent waves crashing all around me, and He reassures me that I belong to Him. He wants me to rest in that and then do what He designed me to do.

One of the things He designed me to do is lead others to Him. I know that now. I'm comfortable with that now. I don't have to wrestle with finding a space in the lifeboat. I already have one in Him. Because He said so. Therefore, it's over. The struggle with belonging, fitting in, figuring out what I am supposed to do is less and less each day. He leads me. Like the Good Shepherd that He is.

Once I quit wrestling with trying to belong in the lifeboat,

I was at peace. I realize that as a counselor it is really hard to fit into a lifeboat anyway. It's too confining, and we get exposed. All of us, including myself. Our shame-based thinking and behaviors, our peace-at-any-price manipulations, our need to control others so we will be okay, our lashing out when we can't. All of it gets exposed.

But one of the gifts God, our Father, gave me so I could be an effective counselor is the gift of discernment. So, when I am with others, I can discern things about them that they might not even know about themselves. I don't say this to brag. Really, it's a burden sometimes. "It's a gift, and a curse," as Monk says. I love that TV series! Monk definitely had the gift of discernment and could see things others didn't notice and therefore solved many crimes. I don't go around solving crimes, but I can help others figure some things out about themselves and their relationships, if they want. Then they have a better idea of the choices they have about whatever is going on in their lives. Believing we have a choice is terribly important.

That's the kind of discernment I'm talking about. But not everyone is comfortable with me being able to do that, and I understand. Nobody likes their issues exposed by somebody else. I don't either. But one thing that others probably don't know about me is that when I "know" something about someone else, I don't judge them for it. Because my Father also gave me a ton of grace and mercy, I can extend it to others. I get that people aren't born the way they are as adults. They are formed into it. But they can change that form when they are ready, with God's help.

Not everyone is ready. In fact, some will never be ready. My own earthly father wasn't ready until the last few months of his life. Mom died just six months before him. Once she passed, he began studying scripture with his sister, Mary, and his brother, Bill. There's a whole story about why he didn't do that before my mother died, but that's for another book.

I noticed a new softness in him when he did. He seemed more approachable than ever before. He was a very wise man, and I would have loved to have been able to go to him with my pain from this latest addiction of relationship/codependency I was wrestling through, but I didn't spend much time with him during this period because I was carrying so much shame about the choices I was making. I couldn't reach out to my dad, even though I now know that he would have tried to help me through it. That's part of the problem. I didn't share with him or mom about what I was going through. I didn't give them a chance to help me. Since he died just six months after Mom did, there was no time to get to know this new part of him. But I rest in knowing that we will have eternity to get to hang out and to truly get to know one another, and I'm okay with that. It's perfect, actually!

I now realize that before this I had actually been a bit scared of my dad because of some childhood experiences. I wrestled with this once I became an adult, and I used pride and avoidance to cover up my fear and shame, which made it hard to draw close to him or to any other authority figure in my life.

Because of my fear I avoided them at all costs! Or if I did have to interact with them, I took a posture of submission that was not genuine. I hate to admit this right now, but it's the truth. I guess I may have matured a little in this now, though, maybe because I have some healthy authority figures in my life, or witness them. My three sons, for example. Okay, as their mother maybe I am a bit biased, but hear me out.

My three sons all parent differently, but they parent wholeheartedly. I mean they are really in their role! They are not absent dads, they are not physically abusive dads, and they are not wimpy dads. They take their role as Dad seriously! And as I watch them develop this role more and more, or maybe as I see their children mature, I see how much work they put into it, but at the same time, I see how much they actually like to hang out with their kids. I never had that growing up, so it seems pretty special to me. They actually plan things with their kids, even at home sometimes. They have game night, video game wars, coffee dates, dinner dates, movie dates, home project dates, or just running-errands dates.

I think that's pretty special considering that I didn't get that. I didn't do it with my kids either, so how did they learn it? I don't know; it's a mystery to me, but maybe it has something to do with who they are married to. I see my three daughters-in-law also take time to hang out with their kids. It always warms my heart. So just a shout-out now to all six of them: Way to go, parents!

So now, back to God as my Father, my Daddy. I am learning to be humble and run to Him more and more. I am learning how much He loves me and wants to protect me. I am also learning that He uses all kinds of ways to provide for me. For instance, I had to meet with a lawyer today. I have a complaint against my license that I have to defend, and not to say too much about that because I can't, but as things have progressed to this point, I see God's leading in it.

He even led me to a Christian lawyer, which is pretty reassuring! Not only that, but I thought I was going to have to pay a retainer fee, and because of some other financial obligations going on in my life right now, I was scrambling to get the money together.

But come to find out today, he doesn't need a retainer fee because I have liability insurance that will cover all his fees. Wow! This has been another lesson in how much God loves me and provides for me. By the way, He also had the case dismissed after just a five-minute phone conference between the licensing board, my lawyer, and myself. He's pretty amazing.

I repented of not doing a very good job of trusting Him in it. It is always hard when a counselor has a complaint filed against them. There is a lot of stress and preparation. But as I came out of it not having to pay a single red cent, I began making some good decisions concerning how I perceive God, money, and His desire to help me in managing it. He's helping me to live the truth that self-control is a fruit of the Holy Spirit; I need His help with this.

So I've begun making some pretty big changes. For instance, I gave up Obamacare and my insurance plan and went for a Christ-centered medical expense share program instead. It's much cheaper and has a much lower deductible. If you haven't checked one out, I highly recommend it! It's based on the story that Jesus told about the Good Samaritan in Luke 10:25–37.

If you aren't familiar with it, here's a recap: This guy gets robbed and beat up and left for dead on the side of the road, and a priest comes along and passes right by him. Not my problem, he thinks. Then this other holier-than-thou guy comes along and does the same thing. But then! Then a Samaritan, from a group of people who are looked down upon by the other religious nuts of the day, comes along and takes the poor guy to town, gets him a room at a motel, and cleans him up. He pays the owner a ton of money to let the guy stay there as long as he needs to in order to get healed up so he can go on his way. Who does that? Well, if you are a *true* Christ-follower, you do! So my point is, God does! He doesn't just say He loves us and is our good Father in heaven. He acts on it! But He uses others to do it too sometimes!

So because I've been accepting God's love and provision for me, I've been able to take off the mask and just be with others without having to perform; finally beginning to believe that I am enough. I am valuable, just because God says I am. I don't have to do things perfectly. I will still be okay and valuable if I mess up. I can't be perfect. I wasn't designed to be perfect. If I'm perfect, I won't need God. (I think He did that on purpose.) But it's for my good, not so He can control me. He knows that I am much better with Him anyway. Even if I could perform perfectly in everything, I would still be lacking Him, and that would be a tragedy!

Before I leave the topic about authority figures, I want to share with you a poem that I wrote for my dad for his birthday one year. It depicts him as I saw him at times, even in my childhood!

DAD

Dads are funny, you know.
They are different wherever you go.
Some are loving and giving;
They make life worth living.

Some are mean and cruel;
They make life more of a duel.
Some rule with the rod;
Others, it just takes a nod.

Mine is unique to me.
I'm glad he always will be.
One thing is for sure:
On him I can count, no matter what does occur.

He supports my every move.
Even if he disagrees, he approves.
He knows I need to find my own way,
Even if I'll pay dearly someday.

Mistakes are a part of life, he believes,
Even when they bring us to our knees.
He knows that they help us to grow.
They are really a friend, not a foe.

This is how he has learned in life,
With lots and lots of strife.
Now he is pretty smart;
I can count on his wise heart.

I just pick up the phone and dial.
There he is, guiding with a smile.
Even when I need to borrow money,
"Got you covered," he says with a smile.

How much better can dads get?
Mine's the best, I bet,
Loving all fourteen of us kids
Even when we were flipping his lid.

Playing music in a band
With Mom and friends all across the land,
I'm proud of my ol' Dad.
He's come a long way since he was a lad.

His relationship with God is growing too.
He knows what it is he has to do.
He guides him with a nod and smile.
He loves my dad and shows him He's with him
every mile.

Questions for Reflection or Small Group Discussion

1. What was your relationship with your father figure like when you were a child? How about now as an adult?

2. Do you have a Father/child relationship with God now? If not, what is keeping you from having one?

3. Have you climbed out of the lifeboat; stopped performing for acceptance?

9

WE NEED OTHERS

I live in Montana. We have some pretty wicked winters, as you've probably heard, or maybe experienced yourself, but when it's above thirty degrees outside, and the wind isn't blowing too cold, I try to go snowshoeing or hiking as much as possible. This past winter I had an opportunity to do so. These times are filled with conversations with my Creator, my Friend, my Counselor, my Daddy!

I heard from Him recently that sometimes it's a good idea, and makes it easier to travel in life, if I follow another's path. As I went hiking today, I was thinking about this some more as I started following deer tracks. It was a lot easier stepping into where they had walked in the deep snow. They left quite an amazing print because it's not just their hoofprint, it includes their leg too. Seriously! Check it out next time you see deer tracks in the deep snow. It made walking much easier.

It reminded me that sometimes I might need a mentor or sponsor, or a trusted friend or counselor who has gone down the same road as me, but is a little ahead and has discovered some truths along the way that could help me. I have tried, at times, to be independent and private when it comes to problems going on in my life, even though I know better. It always goes much better when I reach out and ask for help.

God has sent me several helpers over the years, both in recovery programs and out. One example was when I was attending Al-Anon in 2012. C. helped me tremendously when I was being healed of my codependency addiction. (Thanks so much, C. I still think of you and hear your words of wisdom, even when I don't want to!)

Earlier in my life, there was another person who didn't mind talking about my addictions and my recovery from sexual abuse, my maternal grandmother. We wrote letters back and forth to each other and discussed it, and we talked in person when we could.

You know, even as I think about it now, I realize how hard that must have been for Grandma. She didn't have much schooling when she was growing up, and she had experienced some of her own abuse, as well as losing her mom when she was born. Her mom died in childbirth, and then shortly after that her dad died.

One year, she told her story by dictating it to her daughter-in-law, my Aunt Mary, as my aunt typed it up. Yes, typed!

On a typewriter. I have a copy of it still. It's a treasure to me for sure.

She told about her birth in 1904 and her childhood and her early years of marriage. As a young girl, she had to work very hard from sunup to sundown. She also shared some of the trials and tribulations she went through when she was first married. She shared how they couldn't even afford a postage stamp, which was two pennies, for a letter to her sisters. She used wooden apple crates that she decorated for cabinets. She also shared about going to church every Sunday in a buckboard wagon, no matter how cold it was on a Canadian winter morning. She described how they would heat bricks in the oven for their feet so they wouldn't freeze along the way!

She continued to work hard all her life. And as she reached her retirement years, even if there wasn't anything that needed done, she still found ways to keep herself busy. She went for walks daily, long walks. She visited her son's used furniture store often and made deals with him to change out her current furniture, just for the sake of change. She danced to the radio and old records to entertain herself. She visited friends and family members and had them over for dinner and cards. And she joined the senior citizen center and participated in many events. She continued to do these things until she developed breast cancer and her time was drawing near to go home to the Lord. She then moved in with my dad and mom, who took care of her until the end.

I'm telling you all this because she was an inspiration to me, and even though her generation never talked about sex, and she couldn't even write the word in the letters she wrote me (instead, she put *XXX*), she was willing to talk with me about the abuse when others wouldn't.

So here I am, fourteen years after her death. Lots has happened since then, but I feel stronger for it. As her hardships and wounds made her stronger, so did mine. Scripture refers to this in Romans 5:3–5: NIV

> Not only that, but we even boast of our afflictions, knowing that affliction produces endurance, and endurance proven character, and proven character hope, and hope does not disappoint, because the love of God has been poured out into our hearts through the Holy Spirit that has been given to us.

She was a great mentor in this way, and I greatly appreciate all that she has taught me.

There have been others who have helped me through the years too. After I left my husband in 2008, I was hurting big-time. I needed others to help me walk through this period of life. Besides the grief from the loss of my marriage, my sister and mother died one week apart the next year and then my father six months later. I also temporarily lost an office for my counseling practice, because my office was in our home, as I related earlier. So I had some of the top stressors going on in just a twelve-month period: death of a loved one, times three; loss of home, loss of job, and loss of marriage. I needed help!

God provided it through several sources. I found a good professional counselor, I used a lay counseling department at a church, I joined a twelve-step program, and I met regularly with friends for coffee. I knew I couldn't go through all this alone. But in some ways, I still held back. I had struggled all my life to trust others, and this time of life was no exception. Oh, I was open and honest with my professional counselor, but as far as the others went, I wasn't.

I was still caught in some of my codependent relationships, and I didn't want to reveal this to anyone except the counselor. I knew she couldn't tell anyone else, and I didn't want a friendship with her. I knew it didn't work that way, so I held back with everyone but her. And I suffered for it. I was just in too much shame to reveal it. So I carried the burden alone, for the most part.

Until I didn't. I decided to open up to two individuals. The first one was an old friend, but not just in the amount of time we had known each other; she was well advanced in years as well. I had admired this woman from the first time I saw her in mass in the 1970s, when I was still doing drugs and alcohol. She seemed to be at ease with Jesus and in love with Him. I wanted what she had!

I knew she had had some trouble in her life, same as all of us, and I knew she wouldn't judge me. She was a true follower of Jesus. I knew I could trust her. When I opened up to her, she was very supportive. We met several times after this, and she called me at times too, just to let me know she was praying for me.

It was always nice to hear her loving voice. I knew she really cared about me and loved me. I still avoided her at times, especially when I was really feeling bad about myself. But she was always there when I reached out. She passed away a few years ago, but I know I will see her again. But until then I will always be grateful for your support and love, Alice. I love you!

The second person that I decided to open up to was my sister, Janit. She and I had not been close while growing up because I was quite a bit older, and I got married when I was seventeen. Also, she left our parents' house and moved to Arizona when she was eighteen, so we just didn't have the opportunity.

But one day while talking we decided to start praying together on the phone twice a week. It enabled us to really start opening up and trusting one another. We both shared some pretty hard heart stuff. She helped me process the craziness from my unhealthy relationships I was trying to recover from. So just a shout-out to her right now! I love you, Janit! Thank you so much for being there and not judging me, but loving me through it instead. I still enjoy our prayer time together.

I can't close this chapter on how much we need others until I share one more thing. Because of trying to deal with my addictive nature and dealing with a loved one's addictive behaviors, I recently started attending Alcoholics Anonymous again. No, I didn't start drinking again or anything like that, but AA does more than just help a person not drink. It is a spiritual growth program that helps you take an honest look at yourself and make healthy choices. But as I was reminded once more, it is also a fellowship and a place to make lifelong friends.

Because of the COVID-19 virus that is with us currently, a lot of twelve-step groups have moved to phone meetings or online meetings through Zoom. I have joined some of these meetings, and new friendships have begun through this interaction.

At first it was scary. Actually, it still is at times. But these men and women have loved me through it, despite myself! So, I just want to say thanks! You know who you are, and because of anonymity I can't name you. But I really, really appreciate you. Thanks for being there! We aren't meant to do it alone, are we?

Questions for Reflection or Small Group Discussion

1. Do you have or have you ever had a mentor/sponsor in your life? If not, what keeps you from reaching out for one?

2. If you have had or do have a mentor/sponsor, how have they helped you to grow?

3. Have you reached out and thanked them lately?

Epilogue

Redemption and Restoration

I've been praying—praying for redemption and restoration. I wasn't really sure what I meant by that, but apparently, God had an idea. At the time of this writing, it's been ten years since my former husband and I separated, and then divorced. Lots has happened since then.

I received more healing from my relationship/codependency addiction. I bought my own place for the first time. I reopened my private practice. We've had more grandkids born, so we are up to eleven now. Our middle son got remarried. Our oldest grandchild graduated from high school, and our youngest celebrates her second birthday next month. Ron retired, and I will probably be retiring in two years or so and have cut down on my hours. There have been many ups and downs, but mostly ups. There have also been many family celebrations, which we both attended. Now we are friends again, and as of this writing we have become roommates.

Becoming roommates was a miracle in itself. I was on a

date with my eleven-year-old granddaughter. I love to date my grandkids. We have so much fun! Out of the blue, she stated that Grandpa was moving out of the house he had been living in. I asked her where he was moving to. She said she didn't know.

Immediately I was filled with the Spirit, head to toe, and heard the words, *Call him and invite him to move in with you.* I reacted in fear, but I had lived long enough to know that when God tells me to do something, it is always wise to follow His lead because it is for my blessing. So even though I was scared, as soon as I dropped off my granddaughter, I called him. His first words were, "How did you know what I was thinking?"

I didn't know it at the time, but he told me later that he had been working for a pastor building a fence and was walking toward his pickup to get his cell phone to call me and ask if he could rent a room from me. That is God! Pure and simple!

We have talked a lot about what happened during our years together and why the wheels came off the bus for us. We are planning to get remarried, but all in God's prefect timing.

God is the God of redemption and restoration, so we are open to His leading. It could be the beginning of a whole new chapter of our lives. Our three sons and their wives approve and are happy for us, and even though some of my grandkids are too young to remember us together, they are open to Papa and Grandma being together. The older ones are in favor of it too, even though it's been a bit weird for them to start, since they went through the divorce with us.

It's weird for us too, but exciting. We were fifteen and nineteen when we met and dated. We were married a few short years later. I think we might be a bit wiser since then. I think. Maybe. But only God knows for sure. We shall see.

When things get a bit rough and I start beating up on myself again, I try to remember what God promised us in Hebrews 6:19: NIV "We have this hope as an anchor for the soul, firm and secure." Here's another poem I wrote a few years ago about this.

MY ANCHOR

Jesus is my anchor;
My soul is secure and firm.
I can't be put under,
Even when the waves roll and turn.

He is with me always;
I do not need to fear.
He rescued me from the vat
And dried all my tears!

The vat is broken open.
Living water erased all my sin.
Now He is using me
To give others hope in Him.

Question for Reflection or Small Group Discussion

1. How has/is God trying to redeem and restore you and show you that He loves you, just the way you are?

Post Epilogue

I thought I might give an update of what's been happening since I wrote that last chapter. It is now August 2020.

Ron and I did get remarried—last year on the same date as the first time we got married, August 14. What a celebration it was! We included all three sons, our three daughters-in-law, and all eleven grandkids in the ceremony. It made it so precious.

We just celebrated our first anniversary, but we consider it our fortieth anniversary because we were legally married thirty-nine years the first time! So now we've been legally married for forty years!

We celebrated by going to a drive-in theatre because that was what we did on our very first date together in 1969. That was special too.

We talked a bit about what this last year has been like together. We agreed it's been hectic, exciting, scary, and definitely a learning experience! We have had plenty of opportunity to practice self-care and boundaries. We called each other out on the times we would appear to be too needy or too controlling.

We laughed together, prayed together, did chores together, built projects together, did maintenance on the house together, went on trips together, played together, and taught each other some of our likes and dislikes and how some of those have changed over the ten years we were apart. We have become friends as well as a married couple and we are much happier this way.

Our love for each other is more mature than before. We don't expect each other to meet our every need, even our unspoken expectations, and get angry when they don't. That was what we did before. It's one of the reasons we fell apart. Now we realize that no person can meet our every need. We can meet some of our own needs and rely on God and others to meet other needs. But we know now that it is our responsibility, not the other person's, to get those needs met. What a relief. What freedom. What peace!

We are both still amazed that God designed us to be together again. He is amazing! It is a miracle, a true miracle. When we remember this, even in the challenging times, it gives us hope. And we shake our heads and smile, knowing that He truly is in control and loves us very much. And He knows what's best for us.

Wow! What an awesome God we serve!

Oh, and speaking of that, on April 14 of this year, God

performed another miracle. Ron woke up not feeling too well, so he kept checking his blood pressure. I had a date scheduled with that same granddaughter who had told me about him moving out and needing a place to stay in June 2018, and I needed to pick her up at two. He told me to go ahead and go but to keep my phone close in case he needed me to take him in to the doctor. So I did.

At five we were still on our date, but we needed to stop by the house first before we continued on our adventure. Ron said he had talked to his doctor, who had put him on a different medication. I asked Ron if he needed me to go pick it up. He affirmed that he did. Before Zoey and I left again, he came out into the living room and spoke with her for a little bit and then went to change clothes and freshen up.

As he was doing this, Zoey and I were discussing a game we were going to play when we got back. Then we heard a loud thump in the bedroom. I walked in to see what had happened. I found Ron lying on the floor, unable to respond and turning purple. I rushed to call 911, and the operator walked me though how to give him CPR until the ambulance arrived. I'd never performed it on a live human before! It's exhausting, but God gave me strength, and I was able to do it.

Once the emergency personnel arrived, they used a defibrillator on his heart three times and hooked him up with oxygen, but as they loaded him into the ambulance he was still purple. Because of the COVID-19 virus we couldn't stay at the hospital, but my two sons and I rushed there to speak with the doctor and give permission for him to operate on Ron's heart. Then we went home and waited.

After the surgery in which they put two stents in his heart, the surgeon called to say he made it through the surgery okay, but they were going to keep him sedated for two days so his brain could rest and heal. There was no way to tell how much brain damage there was. So we waited, and we prayed.

Ron spent a total of eight days in the hospital, during which time they performed tests, lots of tests. Once he had an MRI, they discovered that his carotid artery was also blocked, 80 percent blocked! That explained his dizziness and low blood pressure. So another surgery was scheduled for later to unblock it.

As I said, there was concern about whether his brain had suffered any damage because of the length of time he had been without sufficient oxygen. Praise be to God, there was hardly any damage at all! He has some trouble with short-term memory, but it is not very noticeable. Everyone was amazed, including the doctors!

I am happy to report that it hasn't slowed him down one bit. He is still able to enjoy fixing things, building things, and helping neighbors and friends with all kinds of projects. Apparently, when God brought us back together, He didn't mean for just a year or two. Of course, none of us knows how much time we have left on this earth, but God was not ready for Ron to go home yet, and for that, we are all very thankful.

Ron was ready to go, though. He shared that he felt himself floating and that it was very peaceful, and others were as well. But God had another plan for him, and He's given us more time together. A second miracle in two short years. God is so good!

As I was thinking about all this, words of gratitude came to mind, and I just had to write them down.

GOD'S DESIGN

God, You are so amazing.
You provide and care for us without fail.
Your plans are bigger and better;
You help us withstand every gale.

You knew we needed time apart to heal.
Life threw us some pretty big boulders.
Our time apart was not wasted;
We learned to lean on Your sure shoulders.

Ten years and our love did not die.
Deep in our hearts it did abide.
We had to let go of the unforgiveness
and anger inside.

You worked it all out; to the surface it did come.
You knew it had to if we were to become one.
Anger makes life quite a mess;
Releasing it is necessary and comes with
forgiveness.

Forgiveness for each other and ourselves;
Forgiveness of others who had hurt us too.
But we were each willing in our own way,
For with willingness, You can make us new.

New creations we are in You,
New creations to live and to love.
Our dormant love came alive again
As it was designed from above!

Bibliography

Ferree, Marnie C. (2010). *No Stones: Women Redeemed from Sexual Addiction* (2nd ed.). Downers Grove, IL: InterVarsity Press.

Hersh, Sharon (2008). *The Last Addiction*. Colorado Springs, CO: WaterBrook Press.

Lasser, Mark (2004). *Healing the Wounds of Sexual Addiction*. Grand Rapids: Zondervan.

Meyer, Joyce (2005). *Approval Addiction*. New York: Time Warner Book Group.

Miller, Donald (2010). *Searching for God Knows What* (2nd ed.). Nashville, TN: Thomas Nelson, Inc.

Ortberg, John (2001). *If You Want to Walk on Water, You've Got to Get Out of the Boat*. Grand Rapids, MI: Zondervan.

Wakin, A., & Vo, D. B. (2008). "Love-variant: The Wakin-Vo I.D.R. Model of Limerence." In Interdisciplinary–Net. 2nd Global Conference; Challenging Intimate Boundaries.

Printed in the United States
By Bookmasters